Fly, Madness, Fly!

by

Lucia Daramus

Grosvenor House
Publishing Limited

This book is published by
Grosvenor House Publishing Ltd
Link House
140 The Broadway, Tolworth, Surrey, KT6 7HT.
www.grosvenorhousepublishing.co.uk

A CIP record for this book
is available from the British Library

ISBN 978-1-78623-058-4

To: Dr. Sally Morgan

English Review: E. Stanley

~~luciadrms@gmail.com~~

philosophantasia@gmail.com

A day room with patients, nurses, doctors, and carers. Everyone gestures. In the room there are armchairs. This is the psychiatric hospital, Wotton Lawn Hospital, Gloucester.

Robert, 79 years old, *patient (singer in choir)*
Jonhson, 76 years old, *patient*
Maria, 68 years old, *patient*
Ian, 56 years old, *patient*
Richard, the man in black, 56 years old, *patient*
Luisse, 28 years old, *patient*
Daniela, 18 years old, *patient*
Pit, the grumpy old man, 79 years old, *patient*
Irina, 30 years old, *patient*
Steven, 40 years old, *nurse*
Lesley, 56 years old, *carer*
Mellany, 29 years old, *nurse*
Liam, 30 years old, *nurse*
Wesley, 37 years old, *carer*
Kelly, 27 years old, *carer*
Dr. Morgan, 40 years old, *psychiatrist*
Peter, 50 years old, *carer*
Tiff, 36 years old, *carer*
Gareth, 30 years old, *nurse*
The young man *nurse*
Merline, *carer*
Vicky, 50 years old, *nurse*
Dr. Rais Ahmed, 50 years old, *psychiatrist*
Serban, *the Irina's husband*
Voice I
Voice II
Voice III
The bad man *(hallucination)*
The children *(the boy and the girl)*
The Doctor I
The Doctor II

The men's rooms, the women's rooms. The doctors' and nurses' office. The day room with TV. The quiet room. The room with books. The kitchen. The windows are large but outside is just the brick wall. A small garden for smoking.

WESLEY: I am Wesley, did you have a lush lunch, Robert?

ROBERT: aircraft, Stonhouse, aircraft, Stonhouse, aircraft, Stonhouse....

WESLEY: I asked you if you had a lush lunch.

ROBERT: ...lush?

WESLEY: ...yes, yes..

ROBERT: The aircraft is lush....

LESLEY: Daniela, keep your doll and come with us.

(*Daniela makes few steps and then she returns. She started to cry. Her obsession is her mother)*

DANIELA: Lesley, mother, mother, my mother, where is my mother?

LESLEY: Your mother, Daniela, will come. She comes every day. You know this.

PIT: You are a bitch, Kelly! Help me with my chair! I am stuck in this stupid chair!

(*Pit has diabetes and paranoia*)

KELLY: Pit, Pit! Be careful, your language is so bad. You have to give us respect! (*Kelly pushing the chair*)

PIT: Oh, you bitch, you hurt me! You caught my leg with varicose veins in the door.

KELLY: Forgive me! It wasn't my intention.

PIT: The women put microphones in my flat. In my hospital room there are microphones too. Fuck you, fuck you, son of a bitch!

(*Luisse comes in the daily room*).

LUISSE: Hello, hello to everyone. My name is Luisse. What is your name?

IRINA: ...my name?

LUISSE: Yes, your name....are you deaf?

IRINA: ....my name...

LUISSE: ...your name?

IRINA: ....is Irina.

LUISSE: very good, Angelica.

IRINA:.....IRINA....

LUISSE: Angelica....What do you want to be in a real life?

IRINA: Am I in a real life, or not? ....a writer, but my name is Irina, not Angelica.

LUISSE: You can be what you want. The life is very important. Is it true? ...you, Angelica!

IRINA: ... maybe....

LUISSE: My family is very precious to me,

because the family is part of the history of the church. My friends are coming to visit me today. My partner is coming too. We are not married. He is Muslim, and I am Christian. Are you listening to me?

IRINA: what?

LUISSE: You are very weird! You are not listening...you don't have eyes contact with me....

IRINA: ...very good, Luisse, very good...

LUISSE: Thank you, Angelica...

IRINA: ...my name is Irina!

LUISSE: I decided, you are Angelica...my mother's cousin is a lawyer, and my cousin is a magistrate...I want to be a psychological counselor...

(Richard comes into the daily room. He believes he is Messiah)

RICHARD: I am Messiah.

LUISSE: You, Messiah? You are a liar....

RICHARD: No, I am Messiah. I will save this world!

ROBERT: Richard, if you are Messiah, I am Mozart.

LUISSE: Shut up, shut up, shut up....you are a singer....lalalalalalalalalalalalalalala

I want to ring home! I want....my family is very important. (*She hits the window with her fist)*

STEVEN: What do you want?
LUISSE: ....my family, I want to ring home...
STEVEN: Go....in your room...now!
LUISSE: I want, I want!
WESLLEY: Steven, Irina has a piece of glass. She can harm herself...
STEVEN: Ok, Weslley, come to Irina.
WESLLEY: Irina, give me the piece of glass.
STEVEN: Do you understand, Irina? It is dangerous! Give me the glass!
IRINA: No, it is mine, it is mine, it is mine.....

(*Steven, trying to grabb it, cuts his hand in the piece of glass*)

STEVEN: Irina, come with me! Do you see? You can harm yourself and you can harm others. It's late...It's time for medication...
MARIA: No, Steven, it's time for TV! It's 11 o'clock....it's evening...
STEVEN: Irina, take your medication, and go to sleep!
PIT: Fuck you, all of you! I need a fag. Fuck you, Robert!
ROBERT: Shit! You harmed me, Pit!
PIT: Shut up, fucking you!

ROBERT: aircraft, Stonhouse, aircraft, Stonhouse, aircraft, Stonhouse....

(Pit urinates in his pants. He falls down from his chair)

ROBERT: ha' ha' ha' you came down in Sena like Celan....

PIT: Like who? Fuck you...

IRINA: You know about Celan...ha'ha'ha'

ROBERT: Yes, I know....

IRINA: You don't! Celan committed suicide... he didn't come down in his pee...He jumped down from the Mirabeau bridge...in Paris.

ROBERT: aircraft, Stonhouse, aircraft, Stonhouse, aircraft, Stonhouse....I know. I wanted to be clever like Pit. What bridgeee....

IRINA: Mirabeau bridge, in Paris.

PIT: Fuck You, Irina with your Ce...ran...

IRINA: Celan, Celan, Paul Celan ....he was a poet...

(*It is 1 am . The patients go to sleep. Irina reading in her room. After 3 hours Irina has hallucinations – the bad man)*

THE BAD MAN: You will die....

IRINA: No, no, no.....go, leave me alone!

THE BAD MAN: You will cut your veins. You

cut a vein before and you will cut again....I know

IRINA: You know nothing....you know nothing....nothing

THE BAD MAN: Why do you repeat the words? ...my words...you are autistic...you are retarded...

IRINA: ....retarded...retarded..

THE BAD MAN: Yes, I told you during your childhood 'you are retarded'...and this is true..

IRINA: You are a bad man, very bad. Leave me alone...leave me alone!

THE LITTLE GIRL: Come on, Irina, I want to play! I want to watch Pinocchio .....

THE LITTLE BOY: ....I want to watch Pinocchio...

THE BOY AND THE GIRL: Pinocchio, Pinocchio...

IRINA: Ok, I really like Pinocchio.

THE BAD MAN: Irina, you are Pinocchio, you are a big liar.

IRINA: You are a stupid man. Do not touch me, bad man, do not touch me!

THE BAD MAN: you will die...

IRINA: go, go, go....

(Irina leaves the room. She goes to the day room. It is 5 o'clock in the morning).

RICHARD: Robert, come, come...it is the sun in middle of the night, the sun...I'm so afraid, I'm so afraid.....the sun...

ROBERT: ...the sun, in the middle of the night?

RICHARD: I created a day, I created a night... the sun is in the middle of the night...this is my desire...is big, and red...

PIT: What kind of sun? I want to see it! You, filth!

ROBERT: Irina, do you see a sun?

IRINA: Stupid, stupid, stupid....leave me alone...(*She coveres her ears with the hands)*

THE VOICE I: You are a beautiful mind. You read a lot, you write, you paint...

THE VOICE II: No, no, no. She is a good actress....

IRINA: Leave me alone...I am nothing...I do not like to be an actress! ....actress....actress!

THE VOICE II: Why not? An actor is clever...

THE VOICE III: She is a big liar

IRINA: You are a big liar....

THE VOICE I: No, she is not a liar, she is an animal, a big animal...she understands perfectly the linguistics...the secret code of language...

IRINA: I like the words, words...

THE VOICE III: She is retarded , she is autistic...

THE VOICE I: Yes, she is autistic, but not stupid....she likes words, she repeats the words, she really likes numbers, she likes to count....

IRINA: I like to count....I like numbers, I like stones , I have a big collection of stones and pebbles...

THE VOICE III: Why don't you look in people eyes? You are retarded....

IRINA: I'am afraid of eyes...Leave me alone.....I'm not stupid, I'm not actress, I'm not big animal....I will go, I will go....(*Irina runs upstairs. She cries)*

PETER: Irina, come! Come with me in the day room. What are you doing upstairs?

(Irina is crying)

PETER: Look at me! I need to have eye contact with you!

IRINA: *(...nothing)*

STEVEN: Irina, come....you must take haloperidol, you are very anxious.

IRINA: I don't want!

STEVEN: Take it! If not, you will have an injection!

IRINA: No....no medications, no injection! My voices, I wanted to find these voices....

STEVEN: Of course! You must take medication! Come on, open your mouth! Look at me, Irina! Ok!

(*The two nurses come and take Irina)*

STEVEN: Ok, now it's time for injection! Look after her!

IRINA: No, no, no! Leave me! Leave me...

.....

(*It is a new day. The patients are in the day room. They watch TV, dance, and play games....)*

PIT: You, stupid, I do not take paracetamol, I do not take medication from you....go...

MELLANY: Take it! Pit, come on, take it! You are a gentleman, you are not a child...ok?

PIT: You, bitch!

MELLANY: You are very grumpy, Pit! Why do you use such bad words?

PIT: Your team is experimenting me!

MELLANY: No, Pit. You are wrong!

PIT: Fuck you!

MELLANY: Pit, Pit....this is a procedure, not an experiment. You must take the medication!

PIT: I'm refusing your medication! Women have disappointed me. I'm refusing your medication!

MELLANY: Pit, are you a misogynist?

PIT: I don't like women....

MELLANY: Come on, Pit. I will stay with you....You must take your medication!

PIT: No, no, no...

MELLANY: Come on...ok, good...You have to take an antibiotic for your varicose veins.

PIT: Weslley, give me a cigar and put me on my chair.

WESLLEY: Please, Pit, please....

PIT: Bitch!

WESLLEY: Pit, control yourself!

PIT: Bitch! Bitch! Bitch....

WESLLEY: Pit! It is dirty in this room, I have to clean....

PIT: Weslley, God looks at you....help me...

(Maria has diarrhea and the poo is dropped everywhere)

PIT: Maria, stupid cow! It smells of poo!

MELLANY: Pit, you are malicious! Maria drops poo, but you pee everywhere.

ROBERT: Today is Tuesday ,... Thursday?

PIT: Fuck you! Mellany, are you proud of you?

MELLANY: I am comfortable with myself.
PIT: I believe in the Universe.
LUISSE: Are you a manager?
MELLANY: No...
LUISSE: Are you a doctor?
MELLANY: No...
LUISSE: Who are you? What is your name?
MELLANY: I am a nurse.
LUISSE: ....and your name?
MELLANY: My name is Mellany. What is your problem?
LUISSE: (*She shouts to Mellany)* I have itchiness on my belly!
MELLANY: Go in your room. I will let the doctor know...
LUISSE: No, No....open the door!

(*Irina talks to herself)*

IRINA:
I am in the dark
the death pushes me
the light is in my soul
Who will see it?
I play of life and death
the trees claws bite me
do not cry when I die
I play of Sylvia Plath

I am Sylvia Plath.
I live in a continual numbness
I enter in my mind like a lioness
I tore myself on the inside
I hurt myself, I do not know to cry
I will soon die, soon
I play of Sylvia Plath
I am Sylvia Plath.

(It is lunch time.)

DANIELA: Where is my mother? ...my mother...I need my mum. I want to wash my hands. My hands are dirty.

KELLEY : Your mum will come. Oh, your food is on the floor. It's ok, Daniela, it's ok... (Daniela has dropped the food).

DANIELA: No, no....my mum, my mum...

KELLEY: Irina, come here, come, come...in lunch room.

IRINA: *(She is silent. She goes to quiet room alone)*

KELLEY: Irina, why do you ignore me? I said come here in lunch room. Why do you prefer to stay alone?

IRINA: *(She is silent)*

KELLEY: Irina, look at me. I need to have eye contact with you. You refuse to speak, you refuse to have eye contact, you prefer to stay alone, you speak to yourself, you are like an autistic girl...

IRINA: (*silently)* It is so boring, so so boring... (*She harms herself, she slaps her stomach)*.... But I'm reading...

VOICE I: Is this enough? I said to you, you have a beautiful mind.

IRINA: It is so boring in the hospital....

VOICE I: Why?

IRINA: ….the books from the hospital are very stupid, so romantic....like a soap...

VOICE I: You are an actress, a big actress....

IRINA: Leave me alone! I am not an actress...

VOICE III : She is not an actress. You are a liar. A beautiful liar. In our language this means you are an autistic girl who lies.

IRINA: You are a liar. And you are very stupid...

VOICE III. No, no, no...liar autistic girl. This is something new. I told you when you were just a little girl: 'you are retarded, autistic..'

IRINA: (*She covers her ears with her hands. She starts crying , and goes upstairs)*.

VOICE III: Cut your veins!

IRINA: Why?

VOICE III: Cut your veins, cut your veins, cut your veins.....

IRINA: Shut up!

VOICE II: A famous writer commits suicide... you are a writer.....

VOICE I: Good, very good...you smashed the mug ….now you …

IRINA: Shut up....(*Irina makes an attempt to cut her vein but it is only superficial)*(*Steven comes in with Dr Morgan)*

STEVEN: What's happened, Irina?! Come, let me treat your wound.

DR. MORGAN: Irina, I am doctor Morgan. I need to see your wound. Show me your hands.

IRINA: (*She is silent. She stretches her hands to doctor Morgan)*

DR. MORGAN: Irina, if you cut your vein again, if you go upstairs, from day room, you will stay in hospital a long, long time...

IRINA: (*She is silent)*

DR. MORGAN: People from Crisis Team have been here to see you. What kind of conversation did you have?

IRINA: They asked me if I wanted to go home. I said yes, but in my home there are microphones, video-cameras, and nanotechnology...I will stay in forest.

DR. MORGAN: Which forest?

IRINA: ….a forest near Stroud.

DR. MORGAN: Why in a forest, but not in a building?

IRINA: Because in a building there is an energy source.

DR. MORGAN: I understand, Irina, I understand....

(It is evening. The patients are in the day room)

MARIA: Hello, Pit.

PIT: What do you want from me, Maria? I hate women. Fuck you, fuck you doctor Morgan. Go to hell all of you....women!

MARIA: Thank you, Pit you are very cute.

PIT: Fuck you!

MARIA: Do you want a cigar? I would like to smoke with you.

PIT: Of course, I want a cigar....Have you just found out that the Earth spins?

ROBERT: Ah, Pit, you are a philosopher! Ah, you are a savant!

PIT: You are a stupid, Robert.

(Maria changed her mood. She started to cry....)

MARIA: Pit, If you want a cigar go and take it! Filthy old man!

PIT: Fuck you, Maria! I said the women are stupid, the women are cunning ….
fuck you!

PETER: Pit, do you want some tea?

PIT: Yes. A tea with milk, no sugar.

PETER: Be careful, it is very hot. Drink it! Thank you....Pit...

PIT: Thank you....

PETER: You , Robert, do you want tea?

ROBERT: ... aircraft, Stonhouse, aircraft, Stonhouse, aircraft, Stonhouse....

PIT: Shut up, stupid!

PETER: Pit, be quiet! He is not stupid, he is a singer, but now he is ill.

ROBERT: ...aircraft, Stonhouse, aircraft, Stonhouse, aircraft, Stonhouse....

PIT: ...take it, and shut up! (*Pit throws the tea in Robert's face)*

PETER: Pit, no, no, no!

ROBERT: ...aircraft, Stonhouse, aircraft, Stonhouse, aircraft, Stonhouse....

IRINA: Here it is so boring, so boring....I want to die, I want to die....In the past I had very clever discussions with some professors about stars, about the Universe, about philosophy....quantum physics...

STEVEN: Irina, every man is important not just bookish men.

IRINA: It's so boring....

STEVEN : Listen to music! Do you like music?
IRINA: So, so boring... I want to die....
STEVEN: Irina, when you smashed the mug, were you angry?
IRINA: Yes, angry....
STEVEN: Did you want to die?
IRINA: Yes, and no...
STEVEN: Or yes, or no?
IRINA: Yes and no! I wanted to die, but to be saved...
STEVEN: In your inner self it is something positive...it is good.
IRINA: ...yes, and no....
STEVEN: What do you do when you are angry inside?
IRINA (*She is silent)*....I harm myself....
STEVEN: Did you ever take overdose medications?
IRINA: ....yeees, paracetamol and aspirin....
STEVEN: ...and?
IRINA: I was near death...
STEVEN: ....and?
IRINA: Finally, I had a big problem with my stomach...
STEVEN: You lose your control....
IRINA: No, no, no....this is not schizophrenia....this is about asperger syndrome ...I was...I am very angry when I have a crisis....

STEVEN: Yes? You were diagnosed with autism?

IRINA: ....when I was a child...

STEVEN: ...yes....you are...

IRINA: I harm myself...

STEVEN: ...yes...did you have a speech therapist?

IRINA: ...yes...I learnt to speak with a therapist when I was five....

STEVEN: ...It was a little later....five years old....

IRINA: ...yes, I was speechless ....

STEVEN: Irina, do you hear voices?

IRINA: ....three voices

STEVEN: Do you know these voices?

IRINA: No, two of them are female voices

STEVEN: ....and one?

IRINA: ....is a male voice sometimes or female voice...

STEVEN: Do you have friends?

IRINA: No, I have a problem with social interaction...

STEVEN: Do you have problem when you have interaction with other people?

IRINA: ....yeees....very big problem...

STEVEN: ?

IRINA: I don't know how to have a real conversation....

STEVEN: ....yes, you monopolize the discussion.....

IRINA: ....yeees....I see... that you know...

STEVEN: hahahah .....Irina....I know, of course ....you monopolize the discussions or...

IRINA: ...or I am silent....very silent....

STEVEN: ....you don't have eyes contact.... Why not, Irina?

IRINA: (*She is silent*)

STEVEN: Look at me, look at me , Irina....

IRINA: (*She is silent*)

STEVEN: ...you don't want....it's ok...you can go in your room. It's time for sleep.

(*Irina is in her room*)

THE BAD MAN: You will die tonight.

IRINA: No, no....go, go, go....Steven, come here, inside is the bad man.

THE BAD MAN: hahahahaha...Steven is not real, he is from your imagination.

IRINA: He is real...he is a nurse..

THE BAD MAN: ...no. I am real, because I can touch you, you can touch me....

IRINA: Don't touch me!

THE BAD MAN: You see?

(*Irina goes to the quiet room*)

TIFF: Irina, what are you doing here?

IRINA: Ah, my hands, my hands. You over-stretch my hand! You hurt me, Tiff!

TIFF: Shut up! I's time for sleep, it's 12 am.

IRINA: The bad man is in my room.

TIFF: There's nothing in your room...

IRINA: He is in my room. He said to me to commit suicide.

TIFF: In your room, now! Good! I will lock you in your room!

IRINA: No....no, no...

(Irina harms herself)

IRINA: I want to die, I want to die...

(Irina smashed a mug. With a piece of mug she tries to cut her vein. Wesley enters in her room)

WESLEY: Irina, give me the piece of mug.. good...

(It's a new morning)

JONHSON: Luisse, please, give me the rest of your coca-cola....

LUISSE: Ok, Jonhson, but I drank from this bottle of coca-cola, there isn't much left...

JONHSON: Doesn't matter....I am an old man....I have nothing to lose. I would like to drink coco-cola, but I haven't got money.

PIT: Fuck you, doctor Morgan, fuck you.... You, foreign, what kind of nationality do you have?

IRINA: ...(*she is silent)*

PIT: You, foreign, are you deaf? ....your nationality...

IRINA: ....Romanian

PIT: What are you doing here? Give me the book you're holding!

IRINA: This book?

PIT: ....yes...

IRINA: It is Shakespeare – Sonnets -

PIT: ...I know....

IRINA: ....What do you want with the book?

PIT: Fuck you, give me the book!

IRINA: (*She is annoyed. She gives the book)*

PIT: Very good. It's enough! You don't read anymore! You annoyed me!

IRINA: You annoyed me, too. You are a very grumpy man! Stupid, stupid old man....

JONHSON: I am from room number 3

PIT: I know, I know...you are from room number 3, stupid man

IRINA: You are stupid, Pit. And you are very grumpy, and you are a jackass!

PIT: Fuck you! I will cut your neck.

IRINA: Fuck you, too. You annoyed me! Give me the book! You grumpy face! You are a shit in the rain!

PIT: Fuck, fuck , fuck.....

IRINA: (*she whispers for herself*)

.....*myself and my mother*

my mother had big belly
in her cave I laid 9 months.
god, god confined my gaze
not to look in people's eyes.
even in the womb
god, god gave me to suck lorazepam
occasionally haloperidol.
the mother's belly was a pothole with sleepers.
there, the subway of God walked
when I came out I found other subway
it was connected to god, god.
the underground whistles, sighs, and whistles again.
outside it was like in my mother's womb – darkness -
people say that they see, but they do not see.
I do not watch people, but I can see.
sometimes, when I am angry I beat my head against the wall
the walls are white cobwebs
my head is the tongue of a bell
and my head rings: ding-dang, ding-dang...

everything is left out
how I was abandoned by my mother's womb
god, god has a womb with sleepers for subway
there people linger lonely, and bored, and
they beat their heads against God-wall, and
their heads ring ding-dang, ding-dang...

VOICE I: A beautiful poem. We'll have to celebrate this.

VOICE II: ...yes, to celebrate your poem...

VOICE III: It is a poem about God, I don't like it.

IRINA: It is not about God, it is about madness, modern madness...

VOICE I: ...modern madness...

IRINA: ....yes, there are four types of madness.....sacred madness...

VOICE I: ...and your poem is about modern madness...

VOICE III: No, it's too late for celebrations..., but it's time for death.

VOICE II: No, it's time for a philosophical discussion. In what kind of context did you find sacred madness?

IRINA: In Greek philosophy there are different types of sacred madness.

VOICE I: I know: the prophetic madness, the ritualistic madness, the poetic madness, the erotic madness...

IRINA: ...inspired by Apollo. Plato, in Phaidros, describes four types of madness.

VOICE III: You, what kind of madness do you have – madness of death?

IRINA: ...so stupid!

VOICE III: It's funny.

VOICE II: No, Irina is not funny

VOICE III. I know, she is not funny because she is autistic, she doesn't know the jokes.

IRINA: What?

VOICE II: ' Suppose we repented '

VOICE I: 'Repented what? '

VOICE II: ' Oh....we wouldn't have to go into the details'

VOICE I: ' Our being born? '

IRINA: Stop it, stop it, stop it.....you are clever voices, but you annoy me, because the words are from Waiting for Godot....

VOICE II: Of course, Irina , Waiting for Godot...

VOICE I: Waiting for Godot....

VOICE II: ...so sad

VOICE I: ...yes, so sad....

IRINA: What is so sad?

VOICE II: The men, Estragon and Vladimir, they waited for Godot …

VOICE I: ….and Godot never came...

IRINA: I saw Godot, I talked to him....

JONHSON: I have Alzheimers , but I remember

something. My name is....is...I forgot ….Irina, do you want tea?

IRINA ....no...but if you want tea I will make it...sugar? Milk?

JONHSON: ...2 spoons of sugar.

(Irina prepares the tea...everywhere on the floor is tea, milk , and sugar)

IRINA: ...take it, Jonhson.

JONHSON: Thank you, but I hate the tea....

IRINA: ….you are mad ....everybody heard you said you wanted tea...

JONHSON: ...yes? Give me the tea...

(It is lunch time. Irina has a meeting with doctor Morgan, a social worker, and other psychiatrist.)

DR. MORGAN: Good afternoon, Irina. I am doctor Morgan. This lady is a psychiatrist, and that lady is a social worker. We want to decide something with you. How are things at home?

IRINA: ... in my home there are microphones, video-cameras, nanotechnology in infrared which transmits via satellite.

DR. MORGAN: Tell me who installed all these?

IRINA: The bad man, the doctor from Romania.

DR. MORGAN: ….explain to me...

IRINA: In my childhood I was diagnosed with autism. The doctor, the psychiatrist, was a young doctor. He punished the children, he beat the children...

DR. MORGAN: Did he beat you?

IRINA: ….yeees, and he ….

DR. MORGAN: ….and he what?

IRINA: *(She is silent)*...I can not tell you.....

DR. MORGAN: Why, Irina?

IRINA: *(She is silent)*.

DR. MORGAN: What he wants from you now?

IRINA: He wants to revenge.

DR. MORGAN: why?

IRINA: Because I wrote a book about him, and I published this book, and now he wants to revenge...

DR. MORGAN: Irina, look at me!

IRINA: *(She is silent. She is very anxious)*.

DR. MORGAN: Irina, do you want to say this doctor from Romania monitors you?

IRINA: ...yeeees. I have video-cameras everywhere in my house.

DR. MORGAN: Irina, In Romania did you have video-cameras?

IRINA: Yes. I had a house in Romania and the writers and doctors from Romania entered in my house and put everywhere video-cameras....and I sold the house and I bought an apartment. But the writers and..

DR. MORGAN: ...the writers?

IRINA: Yes, the writers are in connexion with the doctors...because I wrote in my book stories about writers who were in touch with secret police in Communism time...and they want to revenge now...and...

DR. MORGAN: In your new apartment, was it better?

IRINA: No, because some writers and doctors entered in apartment and put....

DR. MORGAN: ….nanotechnology...

IRINA: Yes....

DR. MORGAN: ….and what does Serban say about these?

IRINA: ….my husband for a second believed me. He rung a company with detectives and they checked the apartment....but nothing...

DR. MORGAN: ….nothing...and what do you say about this?

IRINA: The detectives were in connexion with doctors, because the doctors hacked my telephones and my computer.

DR. MORGAN: ....and in Bridlington? Did you live in Bridlington?

IRINA: Yes...the doctor from Romania came

to England, in Bridlington. I saw him face to face, he was in his car.

DR. MORGAN: A Romanian car?

IRINA: Yes, I saw the car with Romanian number, his car, his face...he was in England.....he tried to manipulate the doctor in Bridlington.

DR. MORGAN: ...what doctor?

IRINA: Doctor Jarman ….but she was very kind...

DR. MORGAN: and?

IRINA: In Bridlington the doctors from Romania entered in our apartment....and I said to Serban, and he rung the police, and police from Bridlington tried to collect the fingerprints from my laptop and door.....but again...nothing ….

DR. MORGAN: What do you say now, Irina, about this? And what does Serban say?

IRINA: Serban says about this situations.... it is just my imagination.

DR. MORGAN: Do you believe you can be ill?

IRINA: It is not my imagination, it is true. I saw him, I heard the voices who spoke to me, it is very real...and the children who come each morning are very real.

Dr. Morgan: The children ….want ….?

IRINA: They want to watch Pinocchio

DR. MORGAN: in the morning?

IRINA: Yees, at 3 o'clock every morning...
DR. MORGAN: …. what can you tell me about your voices?
IRINA: I have 3 voices, female and male. One of them is psychologist, one of them is philosopher or philologist, and voice number III is bad man's voice, is a stupid and bad voice. Sometimes these voices talk about my psychological profile. Sometimes I have discussions about books...
DR. MORGAN: The voices talk to you?
IRINA: They talk about me, or talk to me.... These voices say ' I am a beautiful mind ' because I read a lot, I write a lot, I think, and because of this I must die, I must commit suicide like other writers, for example Sylvia Plath....or Virginia Woolf...or...
DR. MORGAN: Do you want to die?
IRINA: I don't know....I suppose yes....
DR. MORGAN: ...I understand, Irina. You can go. We will continue talking...but I have decided: you will be under Section 2 of Mental Health. You can not leave anywhere!

(During *deliberation time Irina wrote a new poem for doctor Morgan).*

IRINA: I wrote a new, very short poem...
DR. MORGAN: It's about you?

IRINA: It's about death...

DR. MORGAN: I will look at it....thank you, Irina.

Suicide is painless
The wind blows in the window of soul
sadness is of lead and cold
sadness is like over dose medication
suicide is painless, is Sylvia Plath
The wind blows in the window of soul
tiny grain of rose drips on my death
it is night. The blood sneaks
from veins via Milky Way
it is night. Empty tomb awaits me.

......

(It's 3 o'clock in the morning. Irina is in the day room. Her nurse, Steven, wants to talk to Irina. They go in the quiet room).

STEVEN: What happened in your mind? What do you do when Serban is at work?

IRINA: (*She is silent*)

STEVEN: Irina, talk to me...what do you do?

IRINA: ...I read, I write, I paint, I listen to music ….and my mind thinks, thinks ...thinks...

STEVEN: I understand that you like animals...

IRINA: ...yes, I really like animals. I had a crow. Her name was Little Crow. I found her in a field. She was shot by our mayor, Funar. There were too many crows in our city. I took the Little Crow from the field, I went with her to the doctor. She suffered two surgical interventions. My Little Crow was very ill. She had depression, because she was very lonely. When she was alone at home, she snatched her feathers. It was blood everywhere in my house because of this. I went again to the vet and she was euthanized. I was very angry because our mayor shot Little Crow.

STEVEN: At this moment do you have any animals to look after them?

IRINA: At this moment no, but I will have a little dog, a Jack Russell or a Labrador.

In the past I had two dogs, very cute dogs. One of them was killed by a neighbour because my puppy ate his chickens. Another dog, Lucky, was rescued from the street. It was raining, and the little dog followed me. I gave him some food, I washed him with shampoo, and he remained with me. But because he became naughty, my husband sent him in a barrel (with holes to have air) in a car to be released somewhere on a field outside the city... I was very, very angry, and I suffered a lot...

I had two other cats, two rabbits – Yoko – and a parrot – Achiles. I really like the birds. I collect informations about birds.

One morning, I left Little Crow free in my field, near my home. The tomcat of my neighbour, Gaspar, ran after my Little Crow, and Lucky, my dog, ran after Gasper and myself after all of them. I wanted to save my Little Crow. My Little Crow was very intelligent.

STEVEN: It is a beautiful story about your Little Crow. Do you want to be a volunteer at an animal centre?

IRINA: ...maybe ….more I would like to have myself an animal...

STEVEN: Thank you, Irina. Maybe you will try to sleep a while.

(It is a new morning. It's time for medication. The patients are in the day room).

MELLANY: Richard, please, open your mouth. I need to see if you swallowed the tablets.

RICHARD: Of course, Mellany, of course... You see, you can not see a fly. When I created the flies, I made this with a reason. And I created you to give medication to the people.

MELLANY: Oh...my God , we have a philosopher here....watch TV, Richard!

RICHARD: TV....TV....

MELLANY: Irina, come here, where are you going? No, no, come here. You are under section 2, you must stay here. Come in our office. Sit down, Irina, sit, sit...Look, Irina, doctor Morgan said it would be better for you to have 15 minutes free. You can have a walk inside of hospital...

DR. MORGAN: Yes, Irina. You will have just 15 minutes free. You can walk in the hospital garden, make sure you don't exceed 15 minutes. After that, you come back. Are you happy with this?

IRINA: Yes, I will go upstairs, to the second floor. You know.....my voices...

MELLANY: You can go in the day room.

RICHARD: You, all of you, if you sinned, I will save you....Johnson, tell me, what kind of sin do you have? Did you immolate your child?

PIT: Fuck you, Richard! Shut up...

ROBERT: What do sins mean? When an aircraft falls who is the sinner?

MARIA: What? aircrafts? I live in a house and never....

PIT: You, Maria, and your stupidity.

ROBERT: aircraft, Stonhouse, aircraft, Stonhouse, aircraft, Stonhouse....

KELLY: Stop it....everybody ! It's better for you to play a game or to watch TV.

IRINA: ...you voices, again? What do you want?

VOICE I: You said to doctor Morgan that in your house were video-cameras everywhere..

IRINA: Yes, it is true...

KELLY: Irina, come with us...you are lonely and you are talking to yourself again....

IRINA: ....it is true, in my houses , in Romania and in England, there were and there still are video-cameras.

VOICE I: Oh, my dear, definitely in your home were Francois Englert and Peter Higgs and they put in your home bosons.

IRINA: ....so funny....No, Einstein and Enrico Fermi put in my home fermions.

VOICE II: Eh...do you have in your room three dimensions?

IRINA: Of course, like space with the charged leptons, neutrinos, and quarks, and, of course, many bosons but everything is a subjectivity.

VOICE II: Like?

IRINA: Like in quantum physics and philosophy...

VOICE I: What?

VOICE III: nonsense ....it is better for you to die.

VOICE II: No, no...I think it is interesting *like in quantum physics and philosophy.*

IRINA: Yes. The uncertain relations and the measurement in quantum theory presume a form of subjectivity. This is a form of philosophical error which is provided by a part of physics.

VOICE II: ...interesting ...I will give you an example of a philosophical error. Two men in two different cities read the same book. These men share the same story and they have a relationship. But these men don't interact.

IRINA: ...this is an example of a quantum relation. Another example of subjective connexion between philosophy and physics is the potentiality.

VOICE II: The potentiality concept of Aristotle?

IRINA: ...yes. Aristotle speaks about the potentiality of seed which can become a plant. This concept is very interesting as a physical process, and as a philosophical process. Because the seed has the capacity of the finality of the plant.

VOICE II: ...yes.. the seed has in itself the biological and informational material of the plant.

IRINA: Do you want to hear about The Basal Equation Of Europe? It is my theory about Europe.

VOICE II: Is it a philosophical theory?

IRINA: Yes, but you will recognize terms from quantum physics.

VOICE II: I don't like the term 'basal'. You have to change this word.

IRINA: I will reflect. But now you pay me atention. The Universe is a Big Whole like a Universal Matrix, but this Big Whole is in a continuous movement.

VOICE II: What is the relation between physics and The Basal Equation Of Europe, your theory?

IRINA: ...just a second. This Big Whole is in a continuous movement and in a continue energetic structuring. I will overcome these physics rules. Europe represents a Whole which suffers mutations. These mutations are in connection with Levels of Reality of Europe. These levels are: Jewish heritage , Christian heritage, Greek heritage, and Latin heritage. Like in physics, Europe is an open system. Its levels of reality interact between them. This interaction stops the death of the big system, Big Whole – Europe -. It is about unity in diversity and diversity through unity. Between these levels of reality there is *non-resistance zone.* This non-resistance zone makes certain the coherence of information between cultural-historical levels of reality.

VOICE II: What is non-resistance zone?
IRINA: The non-resistance zone is an idea of B. Nicolescu, a physicist from Paris. The non-resistance zone belongs to Big Rationality, it is about sacredness.
VOICE II: But, for the first time, Heisenberg spoke about three regions of reality....
IRINA: ....yes, three regions of reality.... Heisenberg.....the physical region, the region of biological phenomenon, the region of religious experience.
VOICE II: This big system, physical system, and cultural – historical system – Europe – the systems can be destroyed?
IRINA: ....yes, if you think about nature and about her mystery – Black energy -....
VOICE I: ...and your equation?
IRINA: Oh....yes...considering our discussion and acording to my thinking, my equation is:

Jewish heritage LA (level A)
non-resistance zone LALB

Christian heritage LB (level B)
non-resistance zone LBLC

Greek heritage LC (level C)
non-resistance zone LCLD

Latin heritage LD (level D)

Z (LALB) LA/LB + Z(LBLC) LB/LC + Z(LCLD) LC/LD = Z^3(LALB^{2}LC^{2}LD) LALBLC / LBLCLD = Z^3(L^{4}AB^{2}C^{2}D) L^{3}ABC / L^{3}BCD

Z= Non-resistance zone

VOICE II: This equation is mine, I dictated it to you in Bridlington, when you were in hospital.

IRINA: I know, I know, but this equation was in my mind. I wrote it on the wall, but it was not finished.

VOICE II: Very interesting. You and I .....we are one.

VOICE III: Where is the truth?

IRINA: The truth... is always in inanity, in chaos..

VOICE III: I am going to kill you...

VOICE II: Is this your theory?

IRINA: Yes, but the counting continues.

PIT: Fuck....you, women!

KELLY: Stop it, Pit!

(Irina has started to read)

PIT: Irina, what are you reading?

IRINA: It's not your business. Every minute you say *fuck you.* To satisfy your curiosity, it's a book about etymology.

PIT: It is an interesting subject. I am interested in etymology.

IRINA: What?

PIT: You can give me a test.

KELLY: Hey , you, do you want to play a game?

PIT: Fuck you, Kelly, I'm in a middle of an interesting conversation with Irina.

KELLY: Sorry, Pit.

IRINA: Why do you use very bad words? What is your problem?

PIT: All of them are stupid.

IRINA: And are you a clever guy?

PIT: I told you, give me a test.

IRINA: Ok. Tell me, the term *sad,* what is its origin?

PIT: hahahaha, it has German origin, of course.

IRINA: A....interesting, but do you know the word in German?

PIT: ...comes from old German.

IRINA: Good, but do you know that its origin is in the Indo – European language and in Proto-Indo-European which is the lost language?

PIT: Interesting, interesting, I never knew

this. What is The Proto- Indo- European language?

IRINA: According to linguists it is the first language in the World.

LUISSE: What are you doing here? What kind of discussion is this? I had art-therapy and I made a collage. Do you want to see it?

PIT: Yes, Luisse, yes.

LUISSE: I want to ring home. Now, I want.... my family is very important to me!

MELLANY: Luisse, shut up .....come, Luisse, come, I need to give you lorazepam.

LUISSE: Lorazepam is not my family!

MELLANY: Take it, take lorazepam.

LUISSE: I want to ring....

(Irina is in her room. She started to cry. A voice says to her to cut her vein)

KELLY: Irina, what's happened? Why are you crying?

IRINA *(She is silent)*

KELLY: Irina!

IRINA: ...my voices...I am so sad, so sad....and depressed.

KELLY: ....the voices....what do they say?

IRINA: ...to commit suicide, to cut my vein, to smash a mug, and....

KELLY: No, Irina, no...you've smashed enough mugs. Don't cut your vein! I will talk to a nurse...Now I need to go.

IRINA: go, go....stupid voice! Leave me alone!

(Irina goes upstairs to the second floor. She smashes a mug, she cuts deeply her vein. The blood is flowing.)

DOCTOR NUMBER I: *(On the first floor)* I was in Spain. It was marvellous. I had a very good weather.

DOCTOR NUMBER II: Where in Spain?

DOCTOR NUMBER I: In Barcelona. Sagrada Familia is a splendid...and the Gaudi gardens...

IRINA: *(From the second floor)* Shut up! I want to die silently.

DOCTOR NUMBER I: Oh....I suppose that is Irina, doctor Morgan's patient.

DOCTOR NUMBER II: I'm going to ring the carers.

KELLY : Irina....You've cut your vein...come, come...

STEVEN: Irina, you've cut your vein deeply. Give me your hand....Why, Irina, why?

DR. MORGAN: Irina, I want to see your wound. It's deep. Did you want to die?

IRINA: My voices....

STEVEN: Ignore them.

IRINA: Everybody hates me, this life is a shit....a big shit....I am nothing...I am so sad, so angry and depressed...

.....

(The time flies. It is night. In the day room Irina and Pit are talking).

IRINA: Why did you take my Shakespeare's book?

PIT: I thought that you couldn't read Shakespeare. You look like a child....but you know a lot...

IRINA: Do you like Sonnets?

PIT: Yes, I know a few Sonnets by heart.

IRINA: Really ?

PIT: Sonnet XLII

' That thou hast her it is not all my grief,
And yet it may be said I loved her dearly;
That she hath thee is of my wailing chief,
A loss in love that touches me more nearly.
Loving offenders thus I will excuse ye:
Thou dost love her, because thou know'st I love her;
And for my sake even so doth she abuse me,
Suffering my friend for my sake to approve her.
If I lose thee, my loss is my love's gain,

And losing her, my friend hath found that loss;
Both find each other, and I lose both twain,
And both for my sake lay on me this cross:
But here's the joy; my friend and I are one;
Sweet flattery! then she loves but me alone. '

IRINA: Amazing, Pit....but why do you use so bad words?

PIT: Because I like it! It is late now. I will go to sleep. Take it, take the Sonnets by Shakespeare.

IRINA: Thank you, Pit.

(Ian comes in daily room. He is in black clothes)

IAN: My name is Ian.

IRINA: *(She is silent)*

IAN: My name is Ian. What is your name?

IRINA: Irina (*she whispers)*

IAN: A... your name is Cezara

IRINA: No, Irina.

(Ian takes a place near Irina, and he touches Irina's hand. Irina is very scared. She pulls the chair away.)

IAN: You are annoying me. I want to touch you.

(*Irina is very scared. Ian moves the flower, he moves the chairs)*

IAN: Where are my cigars? Where are my cigars!? Liam! Liam!

LIAM: Ian, your cigars are in the blue box, but the box is locked.

IAN: Liam, I need my cigars! Now!

LIAM: Calm down! Take a cigar, but you will smoke outside...not in the day room.

(Liam is in his office. Irina is in day room. She has voices, and in her room is the bad man. Ian plays with the cigar. He jumps near Irina, and tries to kiss her on the lips. Irina screams!)

IAN: I just wanted a kiss good night.

IRINA: *(Irina screams).* Liam, he touched me, he touched me.....he tried to kiss me...he touched me...

LIAM: Where did he touch you? Did he kiss you?

IRINA: No, he tried to kiss me, but he touched my hands....I hate somebody to touch me.

LIAM: Irina, come in the quiet room, I need to talk to you....Irina, you have to go in your room for a while.

IRINA: I can not, I can not...in my room ... I believed that the day room is a safe place.... but is not. It's not my fault. It's not my fault....fault....fault...*(Irina screams)*

LIAM: No, Irina, it was not your fault....calm down, Irina, calm down...

IRINA: It's not my fault, it's not my fault.... (*she screams*)....

LIAM: Look, Irina, I will unlock another quiet room. You will stay there. You will be safe there. Good , Irina, good. Stay here.

(*It is 5 o'clock in the morning. Liam talks to Ian)*

LIAM: Ian, your behaviour was so bad....you scared Irina.

IAN: I just wanted a kiss good night....

LIAM: Ian, you know the rules of the hospital. You can not touch anybody. Do you understand?

IAN: Yes, Liam, yes....but Cezara has so blue eyes...

LIAM: Her name is Irina. And you can not touch Irina! Now, you must take Lorazepam. If not, you will have an injection. Which do you choose?

IAN: I'm taking Lorazepam. I will go to sleep.

LIAM: Very good....

......

(*It's 10 o'clock in the morning.)*

DR.MORGAN: Irina, you talked to me about the bad man. He wakes you up very early. Every night you wake up at 2 or 3 am because of the bad man, voices and children.
Can you describe the bad man?

IRINA: Yes. I see him. He is tall, he has moustache, he is near thirty years old.

DR. MORGAN: You told me that this man was from your childhood, and he was a junior doctor looking after you. Is this true?

IRINA: Yes.

DR. MORGAN: Do you realize that what you describe to me now is the same doctor from your past? You have grown up, but he has not. He is young, like in the past. Do you realize that this would be a hallucination?

IRINA: (*she is silent*)

DR. MORGAN: Do you admit that it is possible to be ill?

IRINA: But for me it is very real. I can talk to him, he can touch me...and the children are very real. They want to watch Pinocchio....

DR. MORGAN: Irina, can you explain to me what happened in your childhood?

IRINA: He beat me, he beat the children. He tied me on the bed. I was unable to go to toilet. The bed was made of iron. He tied my hands on the iron bed...(*she is silent*).

DR. MORGAN: ....and ....

IRINA: I can not.....*(she is silent)*....he....

DR. MORGAN: What does he want from you now?

IRINA: I wrote an autobiographical book, and in this book I wrote about him....he wants to revenge.

DR. MORGAN: And the children, what do they want from you? Do you recognize them?

IRINA: It is a girl , it is a boy.

DR. MORGAN: What do they want?

IRINA: ...to play with me, and to watch Pinocchio.

DR. MORGAN: Do you watch Pinocchio?

IRINA: Each morning around 3 am.

DR. MORGAN: What is so special about the second floor? You run to the second floor every day....

IRINA: Your office is there...I heard my voices there...I think that the voices are in connexion with you....I'm hearing the voices now.

D.MORGAN: Yes, Irina, my office is at the second floor, but now I am here with you. I'm talking to you. I want to help you. Do you understand?

IRINA: ...Yes....I think is logic.

DR. MORGAN: I will prescribe you some Depixol.

IRINA: I hope ….I will not.... because of this injection I will not put weight. Piportil was so bad, I put weight....a lot...I will read about Depixol...

DR. MORGAN: I will provide some information about the medication. Thank you, Irina. You can go in the day room.

(Irina goes in her room. She write an email)

Dear Professor Daniel Freeman,
I read your book Paranoia. It was very interesting. I made a review for a cultural magazine. I published this review. Do you remember? Now I sent you a poem about death, about suicide.

Irina

Dear Irina,
Thank you for email. I remember about your review. I hope everything is ok with you, and you are well.
Best regards,

Daniel Freeman

MELLANY: Irina, now we go outside for a walk. We will talk about you.

IRINA: I am happy to go outside for a fresh air. Now?

MELLANY: Yes....come …Why did you cut your vein?

IRINA: If I die or not....doesn't matter....sometimes I am so angry....

MELLANY: What? What do you mean? You ……, you can be replaced, and....?

IRINA: In myself there are two people. One of them wants to be alive, the other one wants to die... what is my reason to be alive? I feel like a person who has killed all the world...

MELLANY: Your thoughts are above my thoughts....do you want to talk with a psychologist?

IRINA: A psychologist...maybe ...words.... words...words...the language is very important....in my mind there are a lot of numbers and images, numbers, numbers, numbers... and words.

MELLANY: Do you like doctor Morgan?

IRINA: I don't know her enough, but I like her because she thinks...I really like her name's etymology. Morgan is an old name from Welsh – *mor = sea,* and *can or gan = white.* Her name have 6 numbers...my name has 5 numbers...

MELLANY: What? Interesting...but think about your problems. You must have trust in us. Did you talk to Steven?

IRINA: Yes...

MELLANY: In our office, we talk with the doctors about everything .....Did you have a discussion with Steven about abuse, about sex...

IRINA: It was just a question ….I refused to...

MELLANY: Why? Irina, he is a nurse....

IRINA: It's so disgusting …..

MELLANY: What?

IRINA: ...sexual relationship....

MELLANY: Maybe a discussion with a psychologist.....

IRINA: Maybe...

MELLANY: Tell me about your childhood.

IRINA: I spent a lot of time in hospital...

MELLANY: Why?

IRINA: I was diagnosed with autism.

(Irina covers her ears with her hands).

MELLANY: You covered your ears. What happened?

IRINA: I don't like sharp sounds....annoying me...the ambulance...

MELLANY: ah...the ambulance ...and?

IRINA: ….and anxious...

MELLANY: did you learn to speak ….

IRINA: ….later...I was 5 year old....and I had a speech therapist.

MELLANY: Do you like this way? Or maybe you would prefer to explore another way....

IRINA: No, no...I don't like to change

anything ...I have a routine, and I like to have a routine, for me is very important.

MELLANY: What happens if you change something?

IRINA: It's like somebody destroys my world. I am very anxious...and angry...

MELLANY: Therefore, you stayed a lot of time in hospital.

IRINA: Yes...in three different hospitals... because I was autistic , and also because I had hepatitis B....A nurse didn't change the needle...

MELLANY: What? Is this possible?

IRINA: ...yes...

MELLANY: ….and your parents?

IRINA? ...I can not talk about them....but I hate...

MELLANY: What do you hate?

IRINA: (*she is silent)*

(Again in hospital. Irina sends an email to Professor Daniel Freeman).

Dear Professor Daniel Freeman,

Unfortunately, I have paranoid schizophrenia and Asperger syndrome. I cut my vein. I wanted to die. I have voices, I have hallucinations, I

see a bad man and two children. These voices are from outside not in my mind. I wake up very early , at 3 am in the morning. I am in a hospital and doctor gives me Abilify, Lorazepam, and Haloperidol.
This is my story. But my mind works, works, works...I'm writing a play about madness. It is my experience. I am a writer. My doctor tries to change the medication.

Irina
Dear Irina,
I'm so sorry you have had a very difficult time. I am glad you wrote. I'm sure that you will make progress if you engage your mind in assertive things. This unsatisfactory period will pass. I hope you will be better.
Daniel Freeman

(It is 2 pm. Irina has a meeting. In quiet room are Irina, Vicky – her home nurse -, Serban , Irina's husband, Steven – the nurse from hospital - and doctor Rais Ahmed. Doctor Morgan is enable to be at this meeting)

VICHY: Irina, dr. Morgan is not available to be with us. She had to replace another doctor from Stroud who is ill. Do you understand?
IRINA: *(she is silent)*

VICKY: Talk, Irina...Doctor Morgan is responsible for Gloucestershire. She is sorry for this situation, but she has sent you doctor Ahmed.

IRINA: *(she is silent. She has tears in her eyes. She is very anxious)*

DR. AHMED: I am doctor Ahmed. I understand your name is Irina. I am glad to meet you.

IRINA: *(She is very anxious).* My psychiatrist is doctor Morgan.

DR. AHMED: Yes, Irina, your psychiatrist is doctor Morgan. But she is not available now. I am here for you. Give me a chance.

(Irina is very silent. She has tears in her eyes. She is very anxious.)

DR AHMED: Today we will talk about your new medication, Depixol. Are you comfortable with it?

IRINA: *(She is silent. Serban intervenes).*

SERBAN: I apologize for interrupting, but I know.... I talked to Irina, and she told me she vomited after Depixol. I am a pharmacist, and I know...

DR. AHMED: Yes. Yes. I'm listening...

SERBAN: Because of Depixol Irina vomits ten minutes after taking the tablet, has diarrhoea....I think it is better for her to try something else.

DR. AHMED: Just ten minutes?

IRINA: *(She is silent)*

DR. AHMED: Would you like me to change your medication?

IRINA: My psychiatrist is doctor Morgan.

DR. ACHMED: Yes, it is doctor Morgan. I will talk about this with doctor Morgan.

IRINA: My psychiatrist is doctor Morgan.

STEVEN: Irina, you must understand that doctor Morgan is unavailable for three weeks. Doctor Ahmed wants to help you. He is a very good doctor. He is here specially for you. You have to collaborate with us.

IRINA: Doctor Morgan is my psychiatrist.

DR. AHMED: It's ok. Let's talk about medication. In the past you had a progress with Piportil. What has happened...?

VICKY: I am her nurse. Irina had Piportil injection and her symptoms were remitted.

DR AHMED: Why did she stop the medication?

IRINA: Because I put weight on my body.

DR. AHMED: I need to have an eye contact with you, Irina.

IRINA: *(She is silent).*

DR. AHMED: This is not a problem. We are able to control your weight. We have two options: to start again Piportil, or to change to a different medication. But for this you must stay in hospital for a while. What do you think about that?

IRINA: I am not a doctor. My psychiatrist is doctor Morgan.

DR. AHMED: I know , Irina, I know...But you can choose.

IRINA: I will do what doctor Morgan says.

DR. AHMED: I understand....If I talk to doctor Morgan and she says Piportil....you...

IRINA: ....yes...

DR. AHMED: Now, talk to me....about your situation. You had a psychiatrist in your childhood?

IRINA: ...yes....and I started to talk when I was 5 years old....

DR. AHMED: We must investigate if you have Asperger Syndrome or if it's just suspected that you have. Do you want to do some tests?

IRINA: Yes, why not....

DR. AHMED: Good, very good. You see, there are some diseases which have the same symptoms....approximately. We don't know if you have schizophrenia. You harm yourself, you cut your veins, you have depression....

IRINA: *(she is silent. She is very anxious)*

DR. AHMED: It could be schizophrenia, it

could be Asperger Syndrome, or Borderline Disorder. We will think about these, or it is possible you have all three diseases..We will see. But, for the moment I will talk to doctor Morgan about Piportil. You will start again.... with Piportil. Is everything ok, Irina?

IRINA: ....yeeees....

DR. AHMED: Tell me now about the bad man. Do you see him?

IRINA: Yes. He can touch me, he can talk to me...he follows me...

DR. AHMED: He can touch you...

IRINA: Yes, he can harm me...he wakes me up very early, at 2, 3 am...

SERBAN: Sorry, doctor Ahmed, but I'm very worried. Irina sleeps just 3 hours per night. Can you prescribe something to help her sleep?

DR. AHMED: We will give her more Zoplicone...Irina, what do you think...the doctor from Romania.... how does he enter your room?

IRINA: He works with doctors and nurses from hospital, this hospital...

DR. AHMED: You say that he works with doctors and nurses from here? But there is another system here. We have no contact with the Romanian medical system.

IRINA: *(She is silent).*

DR. AHMED: Do you trust someone from here?

IRINA: ...yes... doctor Morgan...

DR. AHMED: ….and what about the others? They work for doctor from Romania?

IRINA: ….yeees..

DR AHMED: Tell me, Irina. You have been at home with the Crisis Team, for 30 minutes.

IRINA: Yes....

DR. AHMED: Did you have a good time?

IRINA: I have in my house microphones , video-cameras, nanotechnology...

DR. AHMED: I understand. Do you want to go home?

IRINA: If I go home I will stay in garage, or in forest...

DR. AHMED: Not alone, just for 30 minutes with Crisis Team.

IRINA: If I am not alone....yees...because in my home I have....

DR. AHMED: I know, nanotechnology....

IRINA: Yes.

VICKY: Dr. Morgan said it would be better for her to see a psychologist.

STEVEN: Yes, I have talked to a psychologist....

DR. AHMED: Irina, have you ever seen a psychologist?

IRINA: Yeeees....in Romania. But I played with him....

(*Dr Ahmed laughing*)

DR. AHMED: What kind of game did you play?
IRINA: I wanted to stand out from the crowd...
DR. AHMED: I understand that you write and you have some published books.
IRINA: Yes...
DR. AHMED: Are you writing a play?
IRINA: ....yeeeees , a play about the hospital... My characters are the doctors, nurses, patients, and me.
DR. AHMED: Will I be a character? I am happy...

(*Everybody laughing without Irina*)

DR. AHMED: Do you want to see you a psychologist from here?
IRINA: ....yeees....It's fine....
DR. AHMED: So, we will start with Piportil... We will do some tests, specially for asperger syndrome....
IRINA: If doctor Morgan agrees.
DR. AHMED: That is correct. I will be in touch with her. Thank you, Irina. I am glad to have met you.

(Irina is in her room).

VOICE I: The rope bloomed at the angel's neck who committed suicide...

VOICE II: Oh...yees?

IRINA: Here is a bad smell of hospital, a smell of medication.

VOICE II: Something I can do for you?

IRINA: I tamed a snail...in my dream.

VOICE III: She wants to impress me.

VOICE II: This is her job....to impress people, because she is a writer...

VOICE I: Oh, yes?

VOICE III: No, it's not her job.

VOICE I: What?

VOICE III: She's going mad.

IRINA: How dare you? You are killing me with your bad words.

VOICE III: Come here, Irina.

IRINA: What for?

VOICE III: You'll see.

IRINA: ....go, go away...

VOICE III: I will go, but I'll be back.

IRINA: You are awful.

VOICE II: A little attention, if you please.

IRINA: Yes...?!

VOICE III: You'll catch your death.

IRINA: What?

VOICE III .....your death, death, death....

VOICE II: The imaginary numbers haven't got a representation in the natural world.

IRINA: ....yes...yes...yes..the imaginary numbers are a result of the pure imaginary.

VOICE I: What is an imaginary number?

VOICE II: A squared image gives a reality in mirror ....

IRINA: ....what?

VOICE II: You don't understand because you take everything ad litteram...

IRINA: Oh , yes...

VOICE II: It was a metaphor...

IRINA: '*i*' is a number, imaginary number, which when multiplied by itself gives -1.

VOICE I: This idea was....

IRINA: For the first time Hieronymus Cardanus thought a number, non-existent number ....in his period the name of this number was impossible number.

VOICE II: ....and Descartes?

IRINA: Descartes ....he gave this curious number the imaginary name .... imaginary numbers. And Euler had a contribution too, because he gave a symbol - 'i' - in math.

VOICE I: I don't understand....what is an imaginary number?

IRINA: ...is a complex number. The square of an imaginary number bi is -b ^{2} .....you think that there is such a number – call it ' i ' for imaginary, that could do this:

I X I = -1

VOICE I: It's so funny!

IRINA: yes, imaginary numbers are not numbers that only exist in the brain of weird people .... all numbers in math are imaginary....

VOICE I: and i, what is it?

IRINA: You are boring, I have explained you...

VOICE II: Eh...Eh...the real numbers are all the positive numbers, negative numbers, and zero.

VOICE I: ....and i is a number? So weird!

VOICE II: i is the square root of -1.

VOICE I: We can....

IRINA: Yes, we can calculate, we can elaborate complex numbers...7 + 4i . They are real numbers plus an imaginary number

VOICE I: ....what happens when an imaginary number has an exponent 0?

IRINA: Any number with exponent 0 is 1...

VOICE II: Each power of i can be obtained from the previous power by multiplying it by i:....

IRINA: Well...we have $i^0 = 1$; $i^1 = i$; $i^2 = -1$ etc.

VOICE I: therefore Cardanus.....

IRINA: Yes, Cardanus dreamed the impossible number.....fictive number

VOICE I: But these numbers are real....

IRINA: ....in calculation....

VOICE III: numbers, numbers, numbers....you are weird, Irina...I told you , you are retarded....

VOICE I: Are you a mathematician?

IRINA: No, no, of course not....no, but the numbers are in my brain, numbers and stories, words....every word, every letter has a number....numbers help me to be calm, quiet...when I am very anxious and fussy I count everything.... the thinking without numbers is nothing...

(It is evening. Ian is very agitated. He screams. It is time for medication. The patients are in daily room)

IAN: What is your nationality?

IRINA: Romanian.

IAN: Your name is Nadia?

IRINA: No...

IAN: Ah.....you are not Nadia Comaneci?!

IRINA: No....

IAN: What are you reading? You read all the time...

IRINA: I try to read....you know...my mind...I have not enough concentration....(*she whispers)*

IAN: ...yes, yes...What do you read?

IRINA: When Nietzsche Wept...by Irvin Yalom...(*she whispers*)

IAN: Is it interesting?

IRINA: It is about psychoanalysis...(*she whispers*)

IAN: I've heard of Nietzsche....tell me about the book..

IRINA: …... a meeting between German philosopher and Freud's mentor...(*she whispers*)

IAN: Is the author well-known?

IRINA: Irvin Yalom is a Professor, he is a psychiatrist...and writer...(*she whispers*).

IAN: Pit, you are a great man.

PIT: Eh...for what?

(*Ian screams like a devil. Mellany and Weslley come and put Ian in a chair.*)

PIT: Fuck you...give him something.... Mellany, can't you see he's having a crisis.

Mellany: Pit....your words...now he is in our hands.

PIT: Hanna, last evening I was near your window. I sang to you a serenade...but you nothing..

IRINA: My name is Irina, not Hanna. All of you change my name! Why?!

PIT: A'... your book is about Nietzsche...I know Nietzsche....do you want Shakespeare?

IRINA: No, thank you...but now I'm reading *When Nietzsche Wept.*

(It is time for medication. Everyone receives Zopiclone for sleeping. Irina is in her room. She writes a new email to Professor Freeman).

Dear Professor Daniel Freeman,

I really like the etymology and numbers. The etymology of your name is very interesting.

Daniel is a Hebrew name. In Hebrew the meaning of the name Daniel is : God is my judge. Freeman is a compound name: ''free'' + ''man'' = free born person.

In hospital I feel like in an absurd play; a play by Samuel Beckett, the founder of The Theatre of the Absurd. But I read and write. Today I read an article by Noam Chomsky – ''Corporate Business Models Are Hurting American Universities''. Noam Chomsky is a linguist and philosopher. He is the author of many books and articles.

And I'm reading *When Nietzsche Wept.*

Irina.

(It is a new day.)

STEVEN: Good morning, Irina. Here is some information about borderline disease. Read it now and we will have a discussion about it.

IRINA: Here it reads: *You feel very worried about people abandoning you* ....it is stupid...I am not feeling abandoned ....I like to be alone....people don't like me...

STEVEN: But do you like people?

IRINA: ...What?..

STEVEN: Read, read!

IRINA: so, so stupid...

STEVEN: What?

IRINA: *You don't have a strong sense of who you are* ....I am a writer! I know who I am.

You have suicidal thoughts...

STEVEN: Is it true?

IRINA: Yes, but this symptom is common with another disease...

STEVEN: Yes, that's true...

IRINA: *You feel empty* ...It is again weird, because I am not empty, I am full of creativity. *You have problem with alcohol*....No, ever......I have not appetite for alcohol...and here it is written about sex? So, so stupid....I don't like sex....I didn't have experiences with men...weird, weird....

STEVEN: So....

IRINA: I have not borderline disease... I will write for you some words about me.

STEVEN: Good.

IRINA: I have difficulties in social expression. I have difficulties to maintain a discussion. I have no friends. I am unpredictable. I like to have private activity, like a collection, or reading, or writing...I don't like sounds. I don't like to change anything, it is like somebody stops my world. I have a strong connexion between me and numbers and stories....I like to repeat the activities...I don't understand social rules. I am very anxious when something is new. I have depression. I can not empathize with people. It is very difficult for me to be in a group. I don't like to change things in my home. I have depression when I am not in connexion with very clever people and whereupon I have suicidal thoughts. I like the routine. I like to stand out from the crowd. I have three voices, I see a man, and two children...I see eyes, I see doctors from Romania. …

……

(*It is a new day.*)

MELLANY: Let's go outside for a walk. Why do you just stay in your room? You can go out with somebody, not alone.

IRINA: Outside is very noisy. I don't like the sounds.....

MELLANY: I know. Tell me, Irina, was it ok with Dr. Ahmed?

IRINA: I was very, very anxious.

MELLANY: I heard about that. Do you want to walk this way?

IRINA: I want the same way.

MELLANY: Ok

IRINA: Doctor Ahmed says to do some tests for Asperger Syndrome, and to read about borderline disease.

MELLANY: Do you know what borderline disease is?

IRINA: Steven gave me some informations about, and I read. You feel empty, abandoned, you have problems with your self-image...

MELLANY: ….and?

IRINA: I not agree...I have not borderline disease.

MELLANY: ...you have not...

IRINA: ...no, no. I wrote to Steven a lot of ideas about me.

MELLANY: I know. Why did you cut your

vein? Did you feel empty? Did you feel alone?

IRINA: Because of my voices...And I took over dose medications because of my work... you know, I am a writer....and I failed in a paragraph...

MELLANY: What? That's too much....just for a paragraph you took an overdose of your medication?

IRINA: ....yeees..if you were a writer ....but you don't understand...because you are not a writer.

MELLANY: ...you say that you haven't got borderline disease....

IRINA: Yes...

MELLANY: I agree with you.

IRINA: I know who I am. But do we really know who we are? This is a philosophical problem. It is not about psychiatry, but it's about philosophy.....

This is Steven's idea about borderline disease.

MELLANY: What?

IRINA: Yes...it was Steven's idea...he has influenced doctor Ahmed. But I have not borderline disease. He is a nurse, not a doctor... Let doctor think.

MELLANY: You can go home for 30 minutes with Crisis Team.

IRINA: Yes. But I am very scared at home.

MELLANY: Why, Irina, why?

IRINA: Because of nanotechnology....

MELLANY: I understand....

IRINA: In my room is a big, big eye on the ceiling. This eye talks to me.

MELLANY: Really?

IRINA: Yes....and a flash like in an old photo …

MELLANY: Maybe it's a fire alarm...

IRINA: No, no, no...I painted this eye and the flash...

MELLANY: Do you paint?

IRINA: No, just I play with colours.

MELLANY: I know that you are scared at home, but you need to go home for a short time with somebody. You can't stay for ever in hospital. Otherwise, when you will go home you will be very anxious...

IRINA: I know...

MELLANY: When did you first have a vision, a hallucination?

IRINA: When I was 7 years old. I saw God. He was very old, and very friendly with me. I saw Him on the wall. He talked to me. 'Don't be afraid, He said. I am with you forever.'

MELLANY: ...Interesting. Do you believe in God?

IRINA: Yes.

(It is a new day. Irina reads a book by Elie Wiesel, but her voices invade her).

VOICE I: Do you see, the doctors have no interest in you. You are alone in this world.

IRINA: That's enough!

VOICE II: My memory is ....

VOICE I: What? Do you understand what you read?

IRINA: Leave me alone...

VOICE III: You are alone, very alone...

IRINA: Go, go away ….I'm reading twice, because my mind...

VOICE III: Of course. You just stay with the book in your hands....here nobody reads.

VOICE II: What do you prefer?

IRINA: ...to leave me alone, to read.

VOICE III: I said ….you just stay with the book in your hand...

IRINA: you are stupid, you are a liar. If you want to know, in this morning I wrote an email to Professor Freeman about the book.

VOICE III: ….yees?

VOICE II: It is true, I dictated her this message. I said:

Dear Professor Daniel Freeman,
good morning. I'm reading a book by Elie Wiesel. Wiesel is an American Jewish writer.

I'm reading his book - A Mad Desire to Dance-. It is about Holocaust, about his trauma. He lost his parents in Auschwitz. He has an imagination about his mind. He believes that he is insane. In reality, the psychiatrist demonstrates that he is no insane, but his soul is ill. It is a beautiful book about human suffering.

Irina

VOICE III: Do you believe that Professor Freeman cares about you?

IRINA: I don't know. But I write to him, and to others, and to other very clever people to have intelligent discussions. If not, I feel that everything is absurd, without a meaning.

VOICE III: If everything is without a meaning you can commit suicide. You can cut your vein...

IRINA: Of course....so stupid...do you know something else?

VOICE I: She started to think...

IRINA: ...funny...I hear something ...

VOICE I: Of course, you hear us...

VOICE II: No, no, no...it's your heart or your thoughts.

VOICE III: Where?

VOICE II: In her mind or in her soul...

IRINA: I can not stop! I can not stop!

VOICE II: What?
VOICE I: What?
IRINA: My mind runs...
VOICE II: ...it runs
IRINA: I must go....
VOICE I: Where?
VOICE III: Don't let her go. You are nothing! I am with you forever.
VOICE I: me too...
VOICE II: I am with you...
IRINA: $i^0 = 1; i^1 = i ; i^2 = -1$; $i^0 = 1; i^1 = i ; i^2 = -1$; $i^0 = 1; i^1 = i ; i^2 = -1$.......
VOICE I: The shade eats from Sun...
IRINA: $i^0 = 1; i^1 = i ; i^2 = -1$; $i^0 = 1; i^1 = i ; i^2 = -1$; $i^0 = 1; i^1 = i ; i^2 = -1$.......
VOICE I: The night oppresses the Earth.
VOICE II: What?
IRINA: $i^0 = 1; i^1 = i ; i^2 = -1$; $i^0 = 1; i^1 = i ; i^2 = -1$; $i^0 = 1; i^1 = i ; i^2 = -1$.......The wall decomposes itself in a sheet of roses, my room in the hospital is a garden in which I bury myself. ....my minds tied by Sun.
VOICE III: You are an illustrious rag.
KELLY: Hello, Irina...Irina...It's time for medication. What do you read?
IRINA: ...a book by Elie Wiesel?
KELLY : Who is he?
IRINA: A very known writer.
KELLY: Interesting. I don't read much. I am

interested in fashion, and I really like to help people...

(Irina meets doctor Ahmed on hall.)

IRINA: ....doctor Ahmed!

DR. AHMED: Good -afternoon , Irina.

IRINA: I wrote something about me, after I read about borderline...and..

DR. AHMED: ...and you haven't got borderline disease...

IRINA: ...no, no, no...

DR. AHMED: Mellany gave me what you wrote..I read it very carefully and I think that is better for us to have a new meeting.

IRINA: ….I stay in hospital in the wind...for nothing...

DR. AHMED: What? No, Irina, you are under observation.

IRINA: But I have voices, I require haloperidol, but the nurses refuse to give me these tablets.

DR. AHMED: I know, Irina, I know. You took haloperidol a few hours ago. It's necessary to wait a few hours until you have any more tablets. We don't want you to have an overdose.

IRINA: ...and piportil?

DR. AHMED: Unfortunately, Piportil is no

longer manufactured. We have to have a meeting to talk about a new medication. How do you feel about this?

IRINA: ....yeees...it's fine.

(It is night. It is 12 o'clock. Irina is in her room.)

VOICE I: Hey, Irina, tell me the truth. Did you swallow the sleeping tablet?

IRINA: No, because nobody gave me zopiclone.

VOICE I: Tell me the truth.

IRINA: But it is the truth.

VOICE III: Tonight you will die.

IRINA: Don't speak to me!

VOICE I : What are you doing?

IRINA: I whistle to stars...

VOICE II: You make a noise like an angel.

VOICE I: Like an angel?

VOICE III: No, like a black dust. It's enough for me, you must be dead!

VOICE I: Say something, Irina....

IRINA: *(she is silent).*

VOICE II: You can count the stars....

IRINA: I know, now I know. You are my double image, like in physics....

BAD MAN: Imbecile....

IRINA: You, bad man, you are an imbecile. I can make you disappear....I know, I know...I am a piece of matter in this world, and you must be imaginative antimatter from another world...if we crash we will disintegrate, and I will liberate a huge quantity of energy...

VOICE II: ….nonsense, Irina, nonsense..

IRINA: ...I know, I know ...I am not a galaxy... you know...

VOICE II: ...yes, it is about matter and antimatter...

IRINA: I am sure that someday people will be able to visit a galaxy composed of antimatter....

VOICE I: Are you sure? Because your theory contradicts the laws of physics.

IRINA: I know.....If a piece of matter is in the presence of a piece of antimatter these will disintegrate each other. But, there is a but.... we have no idea about parallel Universes. We just know about this Universe.

VOICE II: I told you about energetic universe, where each form of entity is energy. In this energetic universe there are powerful fluctuations.

IRINA: Is it not a flat space?

VOICE II: No, there are energetic fluctuations.

IRINA: Are these dangerous?

VOICE II: hahahaha...no, no ...these help at

communication. The energetic entities communicate via these energetic fluctuations.

VOICE III: Hey, you....you have the cord from your laptop....you can put it around your neck...

IRINA: ...go...go...

BAD MAN: yes....you wrote a book about me, now you must die …

IRINA: Don't touch me...no...

(Irina goes to the nurses office).

IRINA: I need haloperidol...in my room is the bad man.

GARETH: ….yes , yes...the bad man appears every night. Is it true?

IRINA: Yes...

MERLINE: Come with me, I will make you a hot chocolate.

GARETH: It's not good to give you haloperidol every night.

MERLINE: Yes. She'll go home....and...what will happen during the night?

THE YOUNG MAN NURSE: But doctor Ahmed said to give her haloperidol ....

GARETH: Why is she not sleeping now? Has she been given Zopiclone at ten o'clock ?

MERLINE: Irina did you receive Zopiclone?

IRINA: No

GARETH: I'm giving her the sleeping tablet now.

(Irina shouts at them)

IRINA: I need haloperidol, I have voices...do you understand?

MERLINE: Irina, I know, you are afraid in your room alone, but....

IRINA: shit! I have voices....

MERLINE: You must take Zopiclone for sleeping.

(Irina takes the tablet. After 30 minute the voices have not disappeared).

MERLINE: It's time to go to bed.

IRINA: No, no, no...I still have voices

MERLINE: I will talk to Gareth...

GARETH: Ok, we will give her Haloperidol.

THE YOUNG MAN NURSE: Irina, this is Haloperidol, but after 15 minutes you must go to bed.

(Pit comes in daily room.)

PIT: What happened?

IRINA: (*She is silent*)

PIT: I want a cigar.
GARETH: Pit, go in your room, go to sleep.
PIT: At my age.....the medication doesn't work. I need a cigar....fuck you!

(Pit takes a sit near Irina. He talks to Irina).

PIT: Shakespeare didn't sleep enough....It is better for us to start writing ....hahahahaha...I can not sleep.
IRINA: *(She is silent)*
PIT: Irina, I can't sleep...do you understand? Say something.
IRINA: You can't sleeeeep....
PIT: Yes
IRINA: I don't care.
PIT: You can say ' what the fuck is this?' I'm going to sleep...you must try to sleep too, Irina.
MERLINE: It's time for bed.

(Irina is in her room. She writes a new email)

Dear Professor Daniel Freeman,

Good morning.

I read ''The Myth of Sisyphus'' by Albert Camus. It is a philosophical essay about absurd and suicide. Camus introduces in this essay the idea about absurd. Does the realization of the absurd require suicide? He then characterizes a number of philosophies that describes and attempts to deal with this feeling of the absurd , by Heidegger, Jaspers, Husserl, etc.

Camus shows that there is only a philosophical problem: suicide. Camus opens the essay by asking if this latter conclusion that life is meaningless leads one to commit suicide.

It is an interesting essay. I read it during University, but now I read it again.

Irina

(*It is 3 pm. Irina has a meeting with doctor Ahmed and her husband , Serban.*)

DR. AHMED: We have a meeting today because Irina filled in a screening form for Asperger Syndrome. I will have the score soon, after I see the answers. We consider that Irina has Paranoid Schizophrenia, but I see five Borderline Disorder symptoms.

IRINA: I don't agree. I don't feel alone, I have not chaotic sexual relations with men, I have not appetite for alcohol …

DR. AHMED: Irina, this disorder doesn't blame anybody. Those five symptoms have no connexion with the symptoms you talked about. You had a trauma in the past. You are intelligent and you understand what I said.

SERBAN: I agree with doctor Ahmed.

DR. AHMED: I will find a psychologist in Gloucester who is specialised in Borderline Disorder. They will talk to Irina. Now about medication. We have decided to give you only Haloperidol. For the moment it will be a low dose, but we will increase it, and decrease the other medication – Abilify. If you have visual or auditive hallucinations you can ask for Haloperidol.

IRINA: Everything it's ok for you, but not for me. Last night I had hallucinations and I received Zopiclone for sleep.

DR. AHMED: I understand. You will receive Haloperidol. I have prescribed it for you.

SERBAN: Doctor Ahmed, I am concerned about why Irina receives Zopiclone in the middle of the night? It's better for her to have this medication at 10 or 11 pm.

DR. AHMED: I will find out what happened. I'm going to prescribe Zopiclone ….Now, are you happy, Irina?

IRINA: Yes.

SERBAN: Would it be better for Irina to have Haloperidol by injection in hospital?

DR. AHMED: In future. Now I would like to

see that Irina is responsible, and she takes the tablets...This is what we discussed.

SERBAN: I have another problem, if it's possible....Irina eats only sandwiches, because she doesn't feel comfortable to stay in a queue or to be part of the group, with the others patients....She prefers to eat alone in her room.

DR. AHMED: This is about autism, but we will see....I understand she can not be part of a group....I will see the screening about Asperger Syndrome.

(It's a new night. It's 3 am)

VOICE III: Irina, wake up...cut your vein, cut your vein...

THE BAD MAN: .....you, imbecile, cut your vein...

VOICE II: No, Irina, you must sleep.

VOICE I: It's better for you to read.

MERLINE: What is with you...you can not sleep?

IRINA: In my room is the bad man.

MERLINE: Come with me, I will make you a hot chocolate.

IRINA: No, no, no....my ears...my ears …

MERLINE: What is happening?

IRINA: *(She covers her ears with her hands.*

An alarm in the hospital went off....) My ears, my mind , my mind, my ears....I hate sounds...

MERLINE: It has stopped...how do you feel now?

IRINA: I need Haloperidol...

MERLINE: I will ask Gareth, he's the nurse. Gareth, Irina is hearing voices again, she wants Haloperidol. What do you say?

GARETH: Yes, doctor Ahmed prescribed this tablet for her. Take it, Irina, and then go to bed.

IRINA: *(she is silent. She goes in her room. She writes a new email)*

Dear Professor Daniel Freeman,

It is 3 am. I have voices , but I'm reading Linguistics and Philosophy by Chomsky. I'm reading twice.

Zeno Vendler asserts that " the science of structural linguistics" gives a new technique for analytic philosophy.

Chomsky shows that in every human language surface structures are generated from structures of more abstract sort, which " I will refer to as deep structures, by certain formal operations of a very special kind generally called grammatical transformations".

A grammar of language can be loosely described as a system of rules that expresses the correspondence between sound and meaning in the language. Transformational grammar is a generative grammar of natural language.

Irina

VOICE I: Who is Vendler?

IRINA: An American philosopher

VOICE II: I know. He classified verbs into four categories...

IRINA: ...yeees....which are found in accomplishment , in state, in achievement, and in activity.

VOICE III: ...stupid...

IRINA: Who is stupid, Vendler? It is his theory.....

THE BAD MAN: ....it's enough for me.....die, die, die!

IRINA: $i^0 = 1; i^1 = i ; i^2 = -1 ;\ i^0 = 1; i^1 = i ; i^2 = -1;\ i^0 = 1; i^1 = i ; i^2 = -1$.......

VOICE II: You count again....

VOICE III: You and your numberes.

IRINA: $i^0 = 1; i^1 = i ; i^2 = -1 ;\ i^0 = 1; i^1 = i ; i^2 = -1;\ i^0 = 1; i^1 = i ; i^2 = -1$.......

Irina counts everything....the chairs, the woods in the door, the glasses from window....)...

VOICE II: Is it better now?

IRINA: *(she is silent)*

VOICE I: What are you going?

VOICE II: She's meditating about Dostoievski.

VOICE I: Dostoievski?

IRINA: At the base of Dostoievski's work is not action, but is tragic event.

VOICE I: Are you a tragic event?

THE BAD MAN: ...yes, of course, because she needs to die.

IRINA: shut up!

VOICE II: The man of Dostoievski, as a great sinner, remains in captivity. He is cought in his muddled remembrace of the past.

IRINA: This is the pattern of A. Camus in which the human conscience is unloaded by future and it is own jail for the human being.

VOICE II: It is true. But in Dostoievski sin intervenes. The sin looks the man in the chains of the guilt. The first emotion Raskolnikov experiences, after murder, is loneliness of soul, the nothingness of the being.

VOICE III: What? You are a great sinner...

IRINA: Stupid, nonsense.

VOICE I: A great sinner?

IRINA: At Dostoievski....but the Russian author saves the sinners through the dissimulation of the sin.

VOICE I: What?

VOICE II: Yes. Each man is guilty for all the other people.

IRINA: In this order of ideas, nobody is in a better condition then his fellow.

VOICE II: ....and is not fair for a man to abandon a sinner...

VOICE III: I am a sinner, I am a sinner, I am a siiiiiiiiinner.....

IRINA: $i^0 = 1; i^1 = i ; i^2 = -1$; $i^0 = 1; i^1 = i ; i^2 = -1$; $i^0 = 1; i^1 = i ; i^2 = -1$.......

VOICE III: I am a siiiiiiiinner.....

IRINA: $i^0 = 1; i^1 = i ; i^2 = -1$; $i^0 = 1; i^1 = i ; i^2 = -1$; $i^0 = 1; i^1 = i ; i^2 = -1$.......

VOICE I: I am a vagabond of ideas.

VOICE II: Like in the essay by Zygmunt Bauman?

THE BAD MAN: What are you doing here, Irina? It could be better for you in Romania...

IRINA: Nonsense

VOICE II: She is a vagabond of the cultures. She needs to travel in a lot of cultures....

IRINA: I need to suck from English culture.

THE BAD MAN: nonsense, nonsense.....the English culture is a sedentary culture.

IRINA: Stupid, stupid... I pinch my psyche to be awake.

VOICE III: Why are you happy? You are annoying me.

IRINA: I am happy because of my lips.
VOICE II: What?
IRINA: Yes, my lips are lifted, and because of this I am happy.
VOICE III: You are retarded.
IRINA: You are stupid, and annoying me.
VOICE III: retarded , retarded, retarded....
IRINA: $i^0 = 1; i^1 = i ; i^2 = -1 ; i^0 = 1; i^1 = i ; i^2 = -1; i^0 = 1; i^1 = i ; i^2 = -1$.......
VOICE II: Count, count Irina. Now is that better?

(It's 10 o'clock in the evening. Irina received medication)

STEVEN: What are you doing, Irina?....and your voices?
IRINA: *(She is silent)*
STEVEN: Irina....
IRINA: It's better.
STEVEN: Good. Your tablets, take them, please.
IRINA: *(She is silent)*
STEVEN: How are you getting on with your play?
IRINA: yes, it's fine...
STEVEN: Am I a character? I don't want to be a V.I.P.
IRINA: You are an important character.

STEVEN: Oh , my God! A negative or a positive character?
IRINA: I will see...

(Steven goes in the nurse office. Irina reads)

VOICE I: What are you reading?
IRINA: Leave me alone.....I need to read, but I read twice....my mind...
VOICE I: Yes, but what are you reading?
IRINA: Gordon.
VOICE I: Prose or poetry?
IRINA: Poetry....I like....he was inspired by old Greek literature...

(Steven comes in her room)

STEVEN: Irina, you are talking to yourself... who is in your room?
IRINA: My voices...
STEVEN: Put the book down.....sleep, Irina, sleep. I'll switch off the light...sleep well!

(She falls asleep. After 3 hours the bad man and the voices appear)

THE BAD MAN: Hey, you, Irina.... tonight you will cut your vein.
IRINA: No, Professor Freeman says that I have

good things in my life, I fall in love with a lot of ideas, and it's better to remain just like that.

VOICE III: nonsense....don't pay attention to him, he is a psychologist....What do you want him to say to you?

IRINA: He said to me that ideas and book are positive things in my life...

THE BAD MAN: ....tonight you will die...

(Irina goes to the nurse office. The door is closed. She is very anxious. Pit is in the daily room).

PIT: What is it? You can't sleep?

IRINA: *(She is silent)*

PIT: I fell in love with Mishel. She is 67 years old. I like her...

IRINA: *(She is silent)*

PIT: Are you listening to me?

IRINA: *(She is silent)*

(Steven appears)

STEVEN: What are you doing here, Irina? You can't sleep? You took Zopiclone.

IRINA: *(She is silent)*

STEVEN: Irina...

IRINA: I need Haloperidol

STEVEN: Haloperidol? Cooome on!

IRINA: I have voices and in my room is the bad man.

PIT: Speak to me, Irina. What do the voices say now? I want to help you.

STEVEN: Pit, take care of yourself, leave her alone. You are not a nurse or a doctor.

IRINA: My voices, my mind....

STEVEN: Don't worry about them...I will give you Haloperidol...but after that you must go to sleep.

PIT: I wanted to help you Irina.

IRINA: *(she is silent)*

STEVEN: What are you doing in the day room? Go to bed.

IRINA: I'm waiting .....I'm waiting ....

(*Robert comes in daily room)*

PIT: Good morning, Robert. You can not sleep?

ROBERT : aircraft, Stonhouse, aircraft, Stonhouse, aircraft, Stonhouse....

PIT: I know, I know.....Ah...are you going to the kitchen?

ROBERT: I need a cup of tea.

(*After 30 minutes Irina goes to her room to have a sleep. She sleeps 2 hours)*

It's again 7 o'clock in the morning. Irina is in daily room.

STEVEN: Good morning, Irina. Did you have a good sleep?

IRINA: *(she is silent)*

STEVEN: Smile, Irina, smile. Don't you know to smile?

(Irina smiles)

STEVEN: See? You can smile! What kind of books do you read, just academical books?

IRINA: Yes.

STEVEN: But do you read jokes?

IRINA: No.

STEVEN: Come on. You must have something funny.

IRINA: (she is silent).

STEVEN: Do you like tennis?

IRINA: Yes , I like, but I can not play...

STEVEN: Shame. Today you will talk to Liam, because my shift is finished now, and I'll be here again tonight. But at that time you have to be asleep.

IRINA: (She is silent).

VOICE I: What are you thinking?

IRINA: (She is silent)

VOICE II: You think about God.

VOICE I: What? It is a large and serious debate...

IRINA: The believers say that God exists.

VOICE I: ...yes...

IRINA: Unbelievers say that God doesn't exist.

VOICE II: It's logic.

IRINA: Therefore, the logical factor for God is the belief or the unbelief in something.

VOICE I: It's like God plays dice...

IRINA: No, no, no....every thought must have an argument.

VOICE II: An argument for existence is first cause.

IRINA: yes, yes, in philosophy....everything in the Universe was created. Everything has a cause and this cause is named God.

VOICE II: There is a but..... we have a question. Who made God?

VOICE I: It's a very big question....

IRINA: ....and a relevant question. Who made God? If everything must have a cause, God must have a cause too.

VOICE III: non-sense, non-sense. The truth is about death, and everybody will die, and you will die today....

IRINA: Shut up...I have another question. Who made the law of universal gravitation?

VOICE III: Newton

IRINA: Stupid, stupid....Newton described this law in nature. Human laws can choose their behaviour but natural law not...the changes of natural laws are in the thought of the Universe.

VOICE II: But who is this thought of the Universe?

VOICE I: Yes...who is?

IRINA: If the nature has its own law it means that God has his own law too.

VOICE I: Who created God?

VOICE III: Can anyone see God?

IRINA: No, nobody...it is just a supposition. The scientists and philosophers verified the Universe, and human being and the laws of these...and they concluded that something exists beyond the Universe, beyond human being....and this something was named God...

VOICE I: But now, a lot of scientists say that God doesn't exist.

VOICE II: How do you explain that the world is made perfect for living in it?
And in this world there is the right and the wrong.

IRINA: You say that God exists because in the world there is the right and the wrong?

VOICE II: Yes.

IRINA: This is Kant's idea. This is the ethical law of the Universe.

VOICE I: God is the right or the wrong? Who created the wrong?

IRINA: God is God....The Thought of the Universe is the Thought of the Universe ..... The power of Energy is the power of Energy...

VOICE I: Yes, I understand, but who created This?

IRINA: It's a vicious circle. Are believers delusional? Or God exists or God doesn't exist? I will think about...

(In Irina's room comes Liam.)

LIAM: Tell me, how are you?

IRINA: Last night it was a bad night...I had voices, I saw the bad man...

LIAM: I know. Tell me about your voices...

IRINA: It's so boring....I told about these to the doctor....

LIAM: Yes , I know, but is my job to check again...

IRINA: I have 3 voices...female and male …

LIAM: Do you recognize these voices?

IRINA: No, but one of my voices is perhaps a psychologist, because she talks about my psychological profile. Another one perhaps is a philosopher or a philologist, because she talks to me about ideas and books, and the other one is the bad man's voice.

LIAM: What do they want?

IRINA: The bad man 's voice works with doctors from Romania, especially with the bad man.

LIAM: Do you mean that the bad man controls everything?

IRINA: Yes.

LIAM: Well done, Irina. What is my name?

IRINA: I don't know....

LIAM: My name is Liam.

IRINA: I have a question.

LIAM: ...yes...

IRINA: Why do you give me Abilify? Doctor Ahmed told me that I would receive Haloperidol.

LIAM: Abilify is an anti-psychotic drug. It is better to gradually decrease its dose and to increase the Haloperidol dose. Irina, when you have voices listen to some music or come in day room to be part of the group.... you stay alone all the time.

IRINA: I can not function in a group, I have social problem....

LIAM: I understand....

(Liam goes in his office. Serban comes)

SERBAN: I have a surprise for you.

IRINA: What kind of surprise? I want to see...

SERBAN: Your book, the one you ordered, it has arrived...

IRINA: Thank you...

(Serban goes. The young nurse comes in Irina's room)

THE YOUNG NURSE: Irina, It's time for medication. What do you read?

IRINA: *''The Master and his Emissary'' by Iain McGlichrist.* The author makes distinction between right hemisphere and left hemisphere, and McGlichrist characterizes the history of the culture based on the two hemispheres.

LIAM: It sounds very interesting. Ah...the author is a psychiatrist...

IRINA: ...Yees...it is very interesting because he reminds me about Julian Jaynes who was a psychologist. Jaynes interprets the ancient writings, the tragedies, from the psyhiatrical point of view. He said that gods' voices, whom the people heard, were just some hallucinations of schizophrenia.

LIAM: It's.....

IRINA: But it's a problem. Schizophrenia is a recent illness. We can not force the things.... We can not say that Moses' experiences with God were schizophrenia....

LIAM: That's very interesting...have a nice evening...and remember....if you have hallucinations listen to music.

VOICE III: Irina, throw away your medications....you can't think, you can't work with medication....

VOICE I: Yeees, Irina, throw away your medications....

IRINA: I don't know what to do? Perhaps ......I will keep them in a drawer...

VOICE II: You keep them away? Why?

IRINA: Because I can't work, my mind is very cloudy ....

VOICE I: Who are you?

IRINA: I am a writer.

VOICE II: Why are we frightened by being nothing?

IRINA: I am a writer...

VOICE II: I agree with you....you aspire to eternity?

THE BAD MAN: Hahaahahahaha......What? She has to die.....no eternity....just burial...

VOICE I: There is eternity?

VOICE II: In human brain there is a space of eternity.

IRINA: You asked me if there is an eternity out of time in our brain?

VOICE I: Yes.

VOICE II: It's a serious question.

IRINA: My response is yes, we have in our brain responsible cells for faith. Faith in science , faith in God.....but the final faith is a faith in eternity. We can have faith in eternity of soul or we can have faith in eternity of our energy.

VOICE I: This means that death doesn't exist....

IRINA: In my opinion the death doesn't exist....it is a transformation...and the perspective of science confirms my theory...

Voice II: Like in quantum physics...

VOICE I: But the time exists in death...

VOICE: The death is just a doorstep.

IRINA: There is a time for human being, the human being's time, there is God's time which is an epiphanic time, in which God came down to the human being's time, and there is a time of eternity...

VOICE II: In my opinion the eternity is out of time.

IRINA: This is a speculation.

VOICE I: Heidegger said that time finds its meaning in death...

THE BAD MAN: It is true...you must die..

IRINA: I know the Heidegger's theory, but I am Irina, not Heidegger.

THE BAD MAN: You are retarded, you must die, you must die...

IRINA: Go, go...$i^0 = 1$; $i^1 = i$; $i^2 = -1$; $i^0 = 1$; $i^1 = i$; $i^2 = -1$; $i^0 = 1$; $i^1 = i$; $i^2 = -1$.......

(It's ten o'clock in the morning. Irina has a meeting with doctor Ahmed and Mellany, the nurse).

DR. AHMED: Good morning, Irina. Finally, we have the diagnosis. Tell me how do you feel? Now you've stopped Abilify, you are taking Haloperidol.

IRINA: Over the night I had voices, and I saw the bad man, and I still have voices ....

DR. AHMED: I hope you'll be better with Haloperidol. Now, about Asperger Syndrome....the score of your screening is very high..you have Asperger Syndrome... You need psychotherapy in hospital....Do you agree?

IRINA: ...yeeees. It's fine.

DR. AHMED: You have Paranoid Schizophrenia too.

IRINA: What about Borderline disorder?

DR. AHMED: We plan to investigate that...you will talk about your past with the psychologist. Tell, me, is your work in progress?

IRINA: Yeeees....you, and doctor Morgan, and the nurses are characters.

MELLANY: My God...

DR. AHMED: That is good. Now....tomorrow you will go home to stay over night, just one night. How do you feel about this?

IRINA: I'm afraid. In my home there is nano-technology.... and my voices, and the bad man, I'm afraid.

DR. AHMED: You will have the medication with you, tablets for hallucinations, and tablets for sleeping. Do you want to ask me anything?

IRINA: No

DR. AHMED: Have a nice day.

(Over the night Irina is at home. She can not sleep. She looks at the walls...she is afraid. She returns in hospital)

DR. MORGAN: Hello, Irina.

IRINA: Hello, doctor Morgan.

DR. MORGAN: I was in Stroud for a short time. I understand from doctor Ahmed that you were very anxious. But you must understand that he was in contact with me all the time. Tell me, is the Haloperidol working?

IRINA: woooorking.....but it was an incident....I have voices, I saw bad man , I asked for Haloperidol, but I was rejected...I broke two mugs, and I wanted to cut my vein. I scratched seriously my....

DR. MORGAN: Dou you want to cut your vein because of your anger? I want to see your vein...

IRINA: *(She is silent)*

DR. MORGAN: Irina, you must learn to avoid these voices...You like to read, to write and paint, you read and write, and paint...and listen to music...We have a plan with you. I understand from doctor Ahmed that you were at home for a night.

IRINA: Yees....one night....and half day...

DR. MORGAN: How did you feel at home?

IRINA: It was awful...

DR. MORGAN: Why?

IRINA: Because I couldn't sleep....I had voices, I saw bad man...in my home there is nanotechnology...

DR. MORGAN: In the day time?

IRINA: I was afraid, very afraid because I was alone...

DR. MORGAN: In the night time, when you have hallucinations you can wake up Serban.

IRINA: Why?

DR. MORGAN: Why not? You must have support....

IRINA: But he is not a doctor...

DR. MORGAN: Yes, he is not a doctor, but he is your husband, and he is a pharmacist. We have a plan with you. But now, about your diagnosis, I saw the answers, the score of screening is very high. You have Asperger Syndrome, you have paranoid schizophrenia too. Now about Borderline disorder, there's still a question mark. Some symptoms are very similar with schizophrenia, but we decided you have schizophrenia. What do you think about this?

IRINA: (She is silent)

DR. MORGAN: Look, Irina. We have a plan for you. At the end of this week I will discharge you from hospital. But before this you will go home for two days. You will have support from the Crisis Team. On Friday I will come to your home. What do you say?

IRINA: I am very anxious....It is a new change....but I can not stay in hospital forever...

(It's a new day. In the quiet room are Steven and Irina.)

STEVEN: I am Santa Claus. I have a red shirt.

(STEVEN LAUGHS)

IRINA: (she is silent)

STEVEN: Laugh, Irina, laugh. It was a joke. Never mind. You're going home. How do you feel?

IRINA: I am very anxious.

STEVEN: Why?

IRINA: I will be at home alone.

STEVEN: ....and?

IRINA: Serban works a lot. In my home I have nanotechnology....

STEVEN: You need a dog....to go out...

IRINA: I will stay in home, reading, writing...

STEVEN: Your play is in progress?

IRINA: It is near finishing. In the final I will take an overdose medications and I will die...

STEVEN: How? Explain to me.

IRINA: In my mind I am death.

STEVEN: Do you have a plan?

IRINA: No, no really.

STEVEN: Don't be afraid. On Friday doctor Morgan will come at your home.

IRINA: Yes, I no....

STEVEN: Try to go to the Library in Stroud.

IRINA: I was to that library, but I discovered just stupid book like a soap programme. I hate it.

STEVEN: What?

IRINA: I need philosophical books, manuscripts....

STEVEN: Come on, Irina. Einstein laughed... Please, a smile....you can smile...

(Irina smiles)

STEVEN: You see, you can smile....well done...
(Irina goes to home. She spent time just in

house. She painted... It is Friday. Doctor Morgan and Vicky visit Irina)

DR. MORGAN: Hello, Irina. How do you feel at home?

IRINA: I am very anxious. I have voices...and I forget to take my medications.

DR. MORGAN: ...you forgot to take your medication...This is not very good...I will speak to the Crisis Team...they will check you. What did you do today?

IRINA: I read a very interesting book about left hemisphere and right hemisphere. I read other book Letters To God. It is a book about Communism in Romania.

DR. MORGAN: Just hard subjects ...nothing to amuse you. Can you concentrate?

IRINA: Not really...I read twice because my mind slides.

DR. MORGAN: I understand...and yesterday?

IRINA: ...yesterday ...it was a very hard day. I forgot to take my tablets...the voices inundated my mind, my house...I wanted to committee suicide ….to take overdose medications, to combine a lot of tablets...

DR. MORGAN: What stopped you?

IRINA: I talked about this with a psychologist on internet. He helped me a lot...

DR. MORGAN: I'm glad you didn't take an overdose. I'm glad you are alive. When you have bad thoughts you can ring to the Crisis Team. They are happy to help you. They work 24 hours and they are here in town. And if necessary they can visit you. They are specialists. Do you have their number?

VICKY: Yes, she has. I put the number in her telephone.

DR. MORGAN: Good. These paintings are your work?

IRINA: Yes.

DR. MORGAN: Very clever and beautiful. Look at this painting...the flowers, which fall on the table, appear to be alive. ….and the self-portrait...Are the people in that picture your parents?

IRINA: They are my spiritual parents , I chose them...he is a gastroenterologist.

DR. MORGAN: Very good , Irina. We are going now. Don't be afraid....you are not alone...a lot of people want to help you, and they are around you. The Crisis team will visit you, to check if everything is all right. Soon you will have an injection with haloperidol. It is not good to forget to take your medications. We will look for a psychologist for you. This is our plan at the moment. What do you say?

IRINA: It's gooooood.

DR. MORGAN: Remember, there is the Crisis

Team. You can ring them at any moment. Take care, Irina.

(Irina remains alone. She is scared . She looks outside after doctor Morgan. Unexpected us two big- white wings appear on Irina's shoulders and she flies.)

Finish

Lightning Source UK Ltd.
Milton Keynes UK
UKHW040827280921
391314UK00001B/210

9 781786 230584